How
to
Drink
at
Christmas

Victoria
Moore

How
to
Drink
at
Christmas

GRANTA

GRANTA
Granta Publications
12 Addison Avenue
London WII 4QR

First published in Great Britain by Granta Books, 2011
Copyright © Victoria Moore, 2009, 2011

Victoria Moore has asserted her moral right under the
Copyright, Designs and Patents Act, 1988, to be identified as
the author of this work.

Parts of this book were first published in *How to Drink* by
Victoria Moore (Granta Books, 2009).

A CIP catalogue record for this book is available from
the British Library.

1 3 5 7 9 10 8 6 4 2
ISBN 978 1 84708 471 2

Text design and illustrations by heredesign.co.uk
Printed in the UK by Butler Tanner & Dennis

For Grandma

CONTENTS

INTRODUCTION..10

 CHRISTMAS STOCKING..............................12

  The christmas drinks cabinet.........................14

    Spirits..14

    Wine...16

    And the rest 19

    Extras 20

  Ice freakery 22

CHRISTMAS IS COMING..................................26

  Glamorous aperitifs for small numbers 29

    The Bramhope...29

    Cranberry and clementine sour.....................30

    Aged rum daiquiri...31

    Sloe gin sour, plus tasting notes
        on four sloe gins...................................32

    Gin and tonic, plus tasting notes on five gins......34

    Sidecar...44

    Your own martini..45

    My martini..47

    Smoky martini...47

    Classic champagne cocktail............................48

    Pousse rapière...50

LARGER PARTIES...51
   Vodka with pomegranate seeds......................52
   Cheesy biscuits...53
   Wintry bellini..54
   Veneziano...55
   Cava-Calva 56
   Sloe gin fizz 56
   Victoria plum..57
   Campari and clementine............................58
   Brandy and ginger refresher......................58
   Mulled wine..59
   Robbie's wassail cup.................................60
   Swedish glögg..62

DRINKS FOR DRIVERS 63
   Cranberry cordial.....................................63
   Red grapefruit and elderflower fizz..............65
   Pavlovian G&T..65
   Fresh, vodka-less Bloody Mary......................66
   Long lemon, lime and ginger........................67
   Spicy apple juice......................................68

RETRO KITSCH 69
   Snowball...69
   Blood and sand..69
   Dark and stormy......................................70

★ CHRISTMAS DAY 72

CHRISTMAS DAY APERITIF 75

HOW TO CHOOSE CHAMPAGNE YOU WILL LIKE 76

CHRISTMAS FOOD WITH DRINK 80

Smoked salmon and champagne 81

Turkey and pinot gris. Or gamay.
Or even pinot noir 82

Goose and claret 83

Christmas pudding and Moscato d'Asti 83

Blue Stilton and port (or have you
thought of Madeira?) 85

Mince pies and a glass of — what? 85

Grandma Moore's sherry trifle 86

♣ BETWEEN FEASTS 88

IN FROM THE COLD: WARMING UP AFTER WALKS ACROSS
FROZEN FIELDS 91

Ginger wine 91

Whisky mac 91

Applebuie 92

Spice and coffee milk 92

Milk and plain hot chocolate 93

Some hot chocolate variations 94

Drinks to chase away a cold 95

Eggnog 96

Brandy Alexander 98

A SIP OF SOMETHING BY THE FIRE......................99

    A word on whisky...................................99

    Cognac versus Armagnac.........................102

    Blazing brandy with red berries..................105

A CHANGE OF PACE 106

  PURITANICAL MOMENTS...............................109

    Rosemary and lemon infusion.....................109

    Lime zest and ginger infusion....................109

    Cucumber and watercress vitamin injection......110

    Grapefruit and passion fruit......................111

    Pomegranate and orange flower smoothie........111

  ICE AND SNOW 112

    How rough do you like your vodka?..............112

    How to taste posh vodka..........................116

    Flavoured vodka...................................118

    Zubrówka with apple juice 119

    Making your own cranberry vodka.................119

    Scandinavian inspiration: aquavit.................121

    Food to eat with neat vodkas and aquavit..........121

    Lychee martini....................................122

ACKNOWLEDGEMENTS...............................124

INDEX..125

NOTE ON DESIGN....................................127

INTRODUCTION

Swizzle sticks at the ready. Christmas is not just the season of goodwill to all men. It is the season of champagne cocktails and sherry, of glittering glasses and the clink of ice, of big parties, family gatherings and glamorous soirées. This book aims to supply ideas and advice on what and how to drink from the moment it all begins in November, when you might want a sneaky cocktail after a present-buying trip or as you come humming out of a carol service on a cold night, through to full-on parties and shouty evenings with friends, to Christmas Day itself, including what to drink with the traditional blowout that is Christmas dinner. But Christmas does not end on 25 December; in the hunkered-down days before the end of the year, when you find yourself milling around the house with friends and family, there's always call for comforting drinks such as thick hot chocolate, spice and coffee milk, or buttered rum. You'll find recipes for all of these, and many more, here. Then, as I'm always loath to give in to the idea that all fun must end once the New Year is out, I've also added some suggestions for January drinking – a change of pace to icy vodka after the richness of the Christmas feasts, as well as a few tisanes and juices to sip in a puritanical moment.

How to Drink at Christmas is based on selected material from *How to Drink*, to which I have added over twenty-five new recipes as well as a guide to choosing champagne to suit your taste, and some notes on which festive food goes well with which wine. You might not think it makes any difference what you drink with smoked fish, say, as long it's cold, white and wet, but I suspect that once you've tried an aged semillon with hot smoked salmon and horseradish, or another startlingly good seasonal pairing of smooth, young port with chocolate mousse cake, you'll be just as hooked as I am.

Here's to a very delicious Christmas, and an intoxicating New Year.

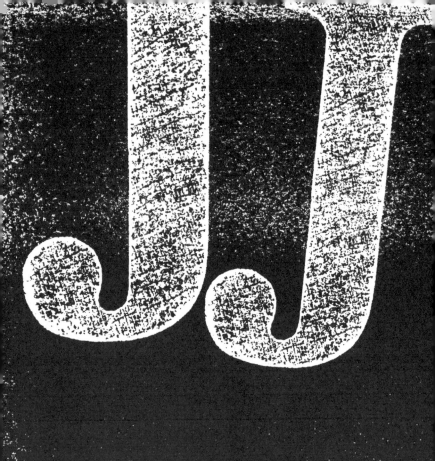

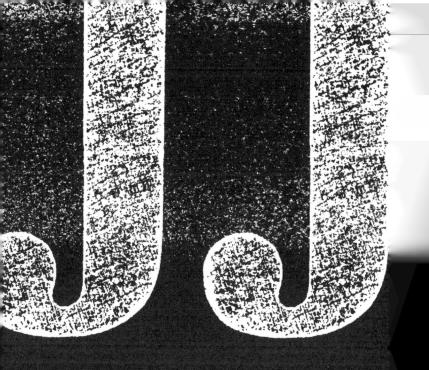

STOCkING

THE CHRISTMAS DRINKS CABINET

You could go on for ever – or at least until practically the last second of 24 December – getting in supplies for Christmas, and still persuade yourself that just one more little bottle of English cider brandy is all you need. And a magnum of champagne. You will know what specialities you need to think about – whether it's the sweet cream sherry for Grandma and the great-aunts, or the rum for Mrs Hoskins from across the road who always pops in on Christmas Eve and likes it with lemonade. Of course, if you're throwing a party or making lots of the recipes from this book, you'll need a proper shopping list, but with the following in the house you ought to be able to make merry and keep friends and family happy, for a few hours at least.

Spirits
Brandy
This is a Christmas essential, as it is likely to make an appearance in brandy butter or the white sauce that goes over the Christmas pudding, and is also an important element in some festive cocktails. I use it in sidecars (see p. 44) and flame it over handfuls of red berries (see p. 105). At the moment I'm using a surprisingly good supermarket own-label Cognac VS for everything except connoisseurs who like it neat. Usually, it's more economical to run two bottles, one for cooking (supermarket own-label, Spanish brandy) and a smoother Cognac (say, H by Hine) for everything else.

Gin

You know that look gin fanatics have – the one which simply does not recognize that you may be a gin-free household? Don't put them through it. Tanqueray Export Strength is my everyday label. I've listed some boutique gins on p. 42–3.

Vodka

To make vodkatinis, vodka and tonic and other cocktails. See p. 112–122 for more on vodka.

Whisky

This is trickiest of all, as whisky drinkers tend to know what they like, and to be quite particular about it. It's useful to have one bottle of cheapish blended Scotch (for toddies, if nothing else) and one of something more special, be it a single malt or otherwise. Highland Park Twelve Years Old is wonderful; utterly complete.

Wine

Wine is always the most personal of choices. You might want to make sure you have a supply of cheap tempranillo for mulling and a few inexpensive bottles of fizz (I almost always go for prosecco over cava). I've included some suggestions for which wine styles might go with which food in the Christmas Day section. Alas, it's impossible to give recommendations for specific wine as they go out of date so quickly, but here's a handful of good places at which to buy it:

Berry Bros. & Rudd (bbr.com)
Britain's oldest wine merchant (the St James's Street cellars are worth checking out if you ever get the chance to attend a lunch there) has one of the most state-of-the-art websites. Try investigating their newly revitalized Italian range. And don't forget the No. 3 London Dry Gin.

hangingditch (hangingditch.com)
A temple to wine in the centre of Manchester, where you can sit and sip a coffee, or wine by the glass (or bottle, for a minimal corkage charge), as you choose what to take home.

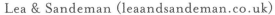

Lea & Sandeman (leaandsandeman.co.uk)

Urbane and London-based, with a notably good selection of grower champagnes (made by small producers who both grow the grapes and make the wines) and Italian wine.

Les Caves de Pyrène (lescaves.co.uk)

Les Caves de Pyrène has pioneered the trend for so-called 'natural wine' in this country. Their main business is supplying wine to restaurants and bars, but if you live near their shop in Artington, not far from Guildford, Surrey, you're in for a treat. With a list that ranges from bloody-tasting marcillac from south-west France to sparkling trebbiano from Italy, you won't get bored.

The Real Wine Company (therealwineco.co.uk)

This is run out of a Portakabin in a garden centre near Slough by a former supermarket buyer who became disillusioned with the approach that multiples take to buying wine and decided to import 'real wine' himself. A very small list, but with some good key wines at £8–£10.

The Wine Society (thewinesociety.com)

There's a one-off charge to become a member of the Wine Society, but once you've paid it you can order their carefully sourced and very keenly priced wines for the rest of your life.

Yapp Brothers (yapp.co.uk)

Founded by Robin Yapp in the late 1960s and now stylishly run by Jason and his stepbrother, Tom Ashworth, Yapp specializes in the Rhône, southern France and Corsica; look here for beautiful, big grenache-based reds and lovely, gently aromatic whites.

Best of the chains

Waitrose and M&S are the supermarkets with the best ranges, and Majestic Wine Warehouse always has some canny buys, as well as being a good place to stock up on champagne.

And the rest

You're going to need . . .

★ Tonic water: ideally you would buy small cans of it, and ideally Schweppes. Yes, even the non-diet version contains some artificial sweetener, but the supermarket own-labels that don't are far too sweet, and Fever-Tree is expensive (see p. 37–8 for more on tonics)

★ A selection of cordials for non-drinkers (Bottlegreen Aromatic Lime and Belvoir Elderflower are excellent)

★ Extra ice-cube trays to ensure a constant supply of ice (see p. 22–5)

★ Angostura bitters

★ Plenty of fresh lemons and limes

★ Fizzy water

★ Beer, of whatever variety the beer drinkers in the house like

Extras

I would also have, in probably this order of priority:

★ Sloe gin (to make sloe gin sours, a pretty unbeatable drink; see p. 32)

★ Gomme syrup (the brand Monin is widely available, or you can make your own by bringing equal volumes of sugar and water to the boil, then leaving to cool, but it's a sticky business)

★ An aged rum (for choice, El Dorado 8 Year Old, but El Dorado 5 Year Old is easier to get hold of)

★ Frozen cranberries (good blitzed with fresh orange juice for a morning livener, and also for making cranberry purée, see p. 63, or the cocktail on p. 30)

★ Red and white vermouth, Cointreau, Campari, Aperol (another Italian bitter)

★ Santa Teresa Rhum Orange (not to make cocktails, but because it is a simply delicious and highly Christmassy rum-based orange liqueur that's gorgeous neat or over ice)

ICE FREAKERY

Is an ice pick essential to cocktail making?
This is the season of blizzards and boots, and putting a shovel in the back of the car in case you get stuck in a snow drift, but until I met a bartender called Kevin Armstrong, it had never occurred to me that anyone living outside the Arctic Circle might feel a piece of climbing gear was a necessary part of their drink-making kit. I still find I can get by without one, but Kevin was adamant that if you are entertaining, 'You *need* an ice pick.'

'Look,' he said, 'making a cocktail requires a phenomenal quantity of ice. People don't always realize that. Sometimes I watch people's faces when I'm making them a drink in the bar. The first thing I do is fill their glass up with ice and I can see they think I'm trying to short-change them on the spirits. I'm not. They get just the same measure, but the drink is better. If you're having a party, you're going to get through a *lot* of ice. You're not going to have enough ice-cube trays, so the easiest way to make it is to freeze water in big roasting trays, then crack it with a baby ice pick. That's what I do at home.'

It would certainly be interesting to see if this explanation washed if you were apprehended by the constabulary on a dark street with an ice pick tucked inside your jacket: 'I am merely on my way to a party where I intend to make gin and tonic for several good friends, officer.'

The ice conversation heated up when Kevin and I discovered we were united in our loathing of those bags of ice you buy in corner shops.

'The cubes have holes in them,' spat Kevin. 'Holes. So they have a huge surface area, melt really quickly, and if you use them in a shaker, they smash to bits and dilute the drink horribly.'

Needless to say, there was more. Kevin prefers ice made with mineral water: 'It gives you an amazing purity and clarity.' It's because it deters the ice from melting that it's best to cram plenty into the glass. More ice cools the drink to a lower temperature, so although there are more cubes, each one melts more slowly, the drink stays both cold and relatively undiluted, and you don't find yourself in that half-panicky, half-miserable state of trying to slurp a cocktail down faster than you really want to in order to enjoy it before it gets tepid and loses its edge.

Kevin was also very specific about the temperature, -28°C, at which he freezes his ice. Ice stored at a lower temperature keeps your drink colder for longer, because as well as absorbing latent heat in the process of transforming from solid to liquid, ice also requires energy — specific heat — to raise its temperature to melting point. In other words, the colder the ice, the colder it will make your drink before even beginning to melt.

The temperature at which ice is frozen also has an aesthetic impact. Peter Barham, a professor of physics at Bristol University, freezes his in the laboratory, using liquid nitrogen, at -196°C. An ice cube made in a domestic freezer would probably have four or five ice crystals in it. At much lower temperatures you get very, very small crystals and lots of them,' says Barham. 'The effect of this is to make the ice opaque.

Ice cubes can appear cloudy for other reasons too. If the freezer door or the freezer compartment in an old-fashioned fridge-freezer is opened a lot, water vapour will condense on top of the ice-cube tray to form a fine frost. And if the water is oygenated (as it will be if run into the trays from a spraying tap), it will also form ice that looks milky rather than clear as a Fox's glacier mint.

Of course, what's most important is to have some sort of ice to hand because even in winter drinks need to be cooled. In the depths of a very cold spell I have been known to open the back door, snap off a couple of icicles and pop them in a glass. And of course there is always the ice-pick.

-28ºC

CHRISTMAS
CHRISTMAS
CHRISTMA
CHRISTMAS
CHRIST M A
CHRISTMA

is COMiNG

is COMiNG

is COMiNG

is coming

is coming

is coming

is coming

is coming

is coming

Two friends of mine have an annual argument about how many Christmas trees there should be in the house. He thinks one in each room plus one for the hall. She thinks that is completely over the top and one in each room would be enough. Who says Christmas is all about children? I've always loved the long, slow build-up of dark evenings spangled with glitter and lights. As it gets darker and colder, and we start tipping bags of raisins and dates into a bucket to make the cakes and, later, putting swags of holly and scented pine up round the fireplace, different kinds of drinks make an appearance too. Cloves and cinnamon sticks come out to mull wine and cider; the whisky stocks are replenished; we might even begin to contemplate a champagne cocktail. This is a time of opulence and luxury (though if budgets are tight, it is amazing how far a couple of bottles of cheap cider can go if you add a few spices and a bit of heat), and an excuse to polish up those martini glasses or open a bottle of something fizzy . . .

GLAMOROUS APERITIFS FOR SMALL NUMBERS

It only takes a few minutes to get the shaker out and make a cocktail, but that's a few minutes you can't afford if you have a couple of dozen thirsty guests baying at the kitchen door. That's why these drinks are better enjoyed in the company of a few close friends. The sloe gin sour is a particular favourite – I love the counterpointing of the sweet, hedgerow taste of the sloe gin against the acidity of the lemon.

The Bramhope

With its orange inflections and smell of molten demerara that rises up like vapour under the heat of a morning Caribbean sun, this tastes like a very sophisticated take on a rum punch. It's also quite a lot stronger than a rum punch, with an edge that makes you sip, not gulp, and its dash of tingly-sweet clementine juice adds a festive note. The drink was invented

50 ml golden rum (I use El Dorado 5 Year Old)
juice of ½ a lime
juice of 3 clementines
large dash Angostura bitters
3 ml gomme syrup

by my friend Joe while staying at another friend's house in Bramhope, West Yorkshire, one year – hence the name – and was tweaked in my kitchen, where several different rums were tested to see which made the best drink.

Put all the ingredients in a shaker with some ice. Shake hard and strain into a martini glass.

Cranberry and clementine sour

*1½ parts cranberry
  purée*
1½ parts vodka
*1 part clementine
  juice*
¾ part Cointreau

A quite delicious short drink that combines two highly seasonal ingredients in a single glass. This began life in my kitchen as I was playing around with the ingredients for a cosmopolitan, the cocktail invented in America in the 1980s and popularized by the TV series *Sex and the City*. The cosmopolitan uses citrus vodka, Cointreau, fresh lime and cranberry juice. I found that using my own cranberry purée (it's simple to make and can also be used for Christmassy non-alcoholic drinks; see p. 63 for the recipe) made a much brighter drink, but that the lime juice clashed with the astringency of the red berries, so I took it out, added freshly squeezed clementine juice to bolster the orange flavour, substituted plain for citrus vodka and – voilà.

Put all the ingredients in a cocktail shaker with lots of ice. Shake hard until mixed and very cold, then double-strain into a martini or small wine glass.

Aged rum daiquiri

The classic daiquiri appears in the 'Summer' chapter of *How to Drink*, but during the winter months I am very partial to a version made using aged rum, which, with its seductive scent of brown sugar, coffee and raisins, makes a much richer drink. I use different proportions of sugar syrup and lime juice when making a daiquiri with aged rum, as the impact of the spirit is much stronger.

2 parts El Dorado 5 Year Old
½ part lime juice
⅜ part gomme syrup

Put all the ingredients in a shaker with lots of ice, shake hard and strain into a martini glass.

Sloe gin sour

50 ml Hayman's
Sloe Gin
20 ml lemon juice
1 tsp egg white

Perhaps you make sloe gin at home. Perhaps you buy it (in which case, see the brief tasting notes below to help you decide which one to go for). Either way, if you agree with me that it's delicious, you will probably be very pleased with this method of drinking it. The use of lemon juice gives an appetizing bite without compromising the earthy, English country lanes taste of the sloes and, as well as chilling it, the ice contributes a slight dilution that helps to make this so refreshing. The egg white is there for texture, giving a more voluptuous drink. It also — and I'm afraid I don't know how the chemistry works here — seems to enhance the sensation of sweetness (or perhaps it suppresses the perception of acidity, which would have the same effect on the overall balance), so if you do leave the egg white out then you may need to add a dash of gomme syrup. In any case, you should taste for sweetness and adjust to your own palate, as some brands of sloe gin are sweeter than others.

Put all the ingredients in a cocktail shaker with lots of ice and shake hard until the cocktail is cold and frothy. Strain into an ice-filled tumbler.

Below are tasting notes for a handful of sloe gins, in case you don't have a jar of your own to hand, and don't miss the recipe for sloe gin fizz on p. 56.

Plymouth Sloe Gin

Made in Devon, this is both widely available and very good; it smells of amarena cherries and almond blossom and has a slightly medicinal nip on the finish.

Hayman's Sloe Gin

This comes from one of Britain's oldest gin families. Hayman Distillers was founded in the nineteenth century by James Burrough, who created Beefeater Gin (though that brand has been sold off). It has a quite wonderful smell – so fragrant, and redolent of pure sloes in all their wild plum glory. To taste, it's plush and on the sweet side, which makes it particularly good for sloe gin sours (though go easy on the added sugar).

Sipsmith Sloe Gin

Sipsmith is a relatively new distiller of small batches of spirits – they also make a barley vodka and a gin, both of them excellent – based in Hammersmith in London. Their sloe gin combines the hawthorn and rich, smoky damson flavours of sloe with superb poise and crispness. A thoroughbred.

Gordon's Sloe Gin

Frankly, a disappointment. I'd expect better from Gordon's, but this tastes confected and artificial and isn't a patch on Plymouth, which is closest to it in price.

Gin and tonic

Some people think there is no need for instruction when it comes to making gin and tonic. Those people are wrong.

A G&T is the most dreadfully traduced of drinks, all too often made too flat, too weak, with one lonely ice cube sweating itself to an early grave and a slice of old lemon floundering on the surface like a corpse, whereas it should be effervescent and bright and so busy with ice that the bubbles have to fight their way up to burst with a splash and a hiss on the top.

To make a good gin and tonic you do not just have to care about every ingredient, you have to be anguished about them.

I never appreciated my husband more than the time he arrived in Italy proudly carrying his own tonic and a set of tumblers (hand-blown, heavy Irish glass) imported from the cupboard at home, because I had warned him that the Schweppes sold in the local shop was virtually flat, and that he might deem the glasses in the rented holiday house inadequate.

The lemon (or lime, which I do sometimes allow in my drink) matters too. There was once a nasty moment at

home when Mum handed me a G&T: I took a sip and said accusingly, 'Has this lemon been in the fridge?' Even though it still looked firm and juicy and the flesh hadn't begun to shrink away from the segment walls, its smell reminded me of clothes that haven't been washed often enough. I kept catching whiffs of unclean air. And as it turned out, I was right, the lemon had been cut into and refrigerated.

I wrote about the incident at the time in a newspaper column, which apparently caused much hilarity among another group of relatives holidaying together in Portugal, who read it online and spent the next fortnight shouting across the villa pool, 'Has this lemon been in the fridge?' But I also received quite a postbag from readers who appeared to share my insanity. A few, I was pleased to see, took it further. Among them was an editor who had offended countless barmen with his regular G&T-ordering routine, which involved shouting, 'We'll have one tonic between two. ONE between TWO,' then wrestling the bottle out of their hands before they could make a mess of it by daring to pour it for him.

Another reader, a professor in a university mechanical engineering department, confessed he was so anxious about running out of fresh lemons that he kept some, sliced 'on day of purchase' and stored between plastic (he was particular that this should not be cling film but something thicker, such as a freezer bag), in plastic containers, in the freezer. 'To be very exacting in extracting the flavour from the fruit,' he wrote, 'simply pour the gin into the glass, add the frozen lemon/lime slices and allow to marinate for 10–15 minutes before putting in the ice and tonic.'

As I say, precisely how you make a gin and tonic is important. So here is a brief guide to each ingredient.

The gin
As a confirmed juniper addict, I like my G&T made with Tanqueray or Gordon's Export (47.3% abv, as against the 37.5% abv of the ordinary stuff, which makes more of a difference than you might think). See p. 42–3 for a more detailed comparison of the different gin brands. The bottle of gin should be kept in the freezer so that the drink is as cold as possible.

The ice cubes
The more ice the better, in my view, and I have recently moved up from three to four cubes. See p. 22–5 for further instructions on ice.

The tonic
Now please pay attention. The tonic must be fizzy and that means using individual cans; large plastic bottles are not good enough, even if they have only just been opened. As for the brand, for me Schweppes is king. I prefer the original Indian Tonic Water because it contains less artificial sweetener than the slimline tonic (even in non-diet Schweppes the

sweetness comes from a combination of sugar and sodium saccharin). Serious G&T aficionados go nuts about artificial sweeteners. The problem is not the health controversies there have been about the likes of aspartame, but the slightly bitter, synthetic aftertaste a finely tuned palate can detect on the finish of the drink. Thus they are the ones you see in the booze warehouses at Calais homing in, not on cases of wine and crates of beer, but on trays of tonic water, because the original Schweppes sold on the Continent, unlike the stuff we get here, contains no artificial sweeteners.

I also like Fever-Tree tonic, which contains no artificial sweeteners (or preservatives) and is expensive but good: in a G& Fever-Tree T you have a much less interrupted view of the gin.

G&T cognoscenti often go on about Waitrose own-brand tonic water, also free of artificial sweeteners, but I don't like it as a tonic – it's confectionery sweet and lacks the requisite astringency. A friend who swears by it cuts it with soda water. Last time I used it, I ended up compensating for the tonic by rattling the gin in a cocktail shaker with the juice of half a lemon, a lot of ice, and the scored rind of the lemon offcuts, just to get some acidity and bitterness back. I can't help feeling that making such a production (in fact, virtually making a Collins not a G&T) may be a step too far.

I scarcely need to mention that the tonic must be chilled.

The citrus fruit

Lime, lemon or both is fine. I tend to use limes only in summer, or if I'm about to eat aromatic food such as Indian or Thai. You should buy lemons that are pale in colour, and ideally a little bit green, as they turn dark as they age. Limes are the opposite: the more yellowy the lime the more juicy it will be. Dark green limes might look the part but they are often dry and hard. I use thick-hewn half-slices or wedges.

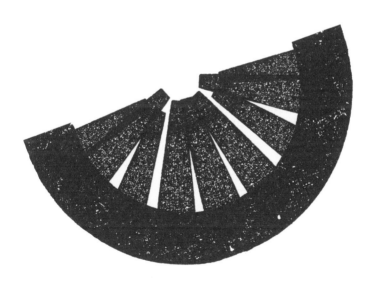

The glass
A heavy tumbler is best. I like ones made from uneven glass. The glass should look as if it understands the gravity of the drink and it should have plenty of space in it. A G&T needs a bit of room. One friend has now finessed his G&T making to the point where he puts the glasses in the freezer for 20 minutes before making the drink. Not strictly necessary, but good, somehow.

Assembling the G&T
Ice goes in the glass first. Then a hunk of citrus fruit, which you should squeeze slightly to release some juice, perhaps even rubbing it lightly round the rim of the glass. Gin goes in next – don't stint. And finally top with tonic to taste.

In the original version of *How to Drink* I included tasting notes for nine different gins. I reproduce the one for my favourite everyday drinking – Tanqueray – here. The other four listed below were either not tasted or not launched in time to be included in that book, but all are superb, so if you have the opportunity to try them, then do.

G&T

Tanqueray

This is a superb gin, aimed squarely at juniper addicts, because it delivers a gloriously emphatic, pine-needlish hit of spice right up front, then follows it through with more juniper. And a bit more. Anchored in root and earth rather than peel and perfume, it has a soft mouth-feel and finesse that match its not inconsiderable bluster. This is the gin that Gordon's lovers flock to once they discover it, and it's one of my favourite all-rounders.

Beefeater 24

The heavy, snazzy bottle is a little off-putting, but this premium offering from Beefeater is extremely good. It's strong on citrus botanicals – you really can smell the orange and grapefruit – and because of that I sometimes add a thick slice of orange rather than lemon to a '24 and tonic'. Those grapefruit notes make this a particularly bracing choice of gin for a martini too – especially if you add a thick blade of grapefruit zest, snapping it in half to release the essential oils from the pores in the skin before dropping it into the viscous liquid.

Sipsmith Gin

Very elegant and composed. As it's relatively delicate, this gin works particularly well with Fever-Tree tonic.

Berry Bros. & Rudd No. 3 London Dry Gin

No. 3 is exceptional, though only for special occasions, as it is not at all cheap. Where many other gins aim to beguile by promoting supporting-role botanicals, No. 3 understands that for anyone involved in a true love affair with gin it is all about the juniper. Thus in No. 3 cardamom pods, orange peel, grapefruit peel, angelica root and coriander seed all serve to amplify and complement the juniper. Patrician and complex.

Gin Mare

Why has no one thought of this before? Gin is defined by the pine-needle scent of the juniper berry, to which distillers add many other botanicals, from cucumber to chamomile, with varying success. This Spanish gin combines juniper with similar Mediterranean, herbal botanicals — rosemary, basil and thyme — as well as arbequina olive. It's truly delicious, savoury and smells like a lungful of tindery Mediterranean scrub, which is a welcome respite from the depths of winter.

Sidecar

1 part freshly squeezed lemon juice
1 part Cointreau
1½ parts Cognac

This is named after a captain whose name is sadly lost to bar-room history, who apparently spent much of the First World War stationed in Paris, tootling, or rather being tootled, around in a motorbike sidecar. As fighting in the trenches worsened, he did his bit by making frequent excursions to a certain bistro, where this drink was created and named after his mode of transport. Apparently the original contained six or seven ingredients. These have since been reduced to three – Cognac, lemon juice and Cointreau – usually mixed in equal parts. David Embury, to whose book *The Fine Art of Mixing Drinks* I am indebted for the sidecar story, objects to this recipe on the grounds of sweetness, though he does allow (somewhat alarmingly) that this is 'not a bad formula for a mid-afternoon drink'. I beg to differ. My version of this cocktail uses a little more brandy than is traditional, but nothing like the quantity Embury suggests, and I find it quite savoury and strong enough for the evening. The presence of brandy makes it particularly suited to winter, and firesides, but it is too good not to make in summer as well. It's important to use a spirit of drinking quality, but there's no need to go expensive.

Shake all three ingredients hard with ice, then strain into martini glasses.

Your own martini

You can decide for yourself which gin you prefer (see p. 42–3 for a discussion of different gin brands), and how much vermouth you wish to add. The real key is that it should all be arctic. Put the glasses in the freezer half an hour before you wish to drink. The spirit should already be in there. For a super-dry martini, it is enough to run a few drops of vermouth round the rim of the glass — so you catch its scent with each sip — and then shake or stir the spirit with ice to loosen its flavour before pouring into the glass and adding, maybe, another drop of vermouth.

Gin (or vodka if your taste runs to a vodkatini; see p. 47)

vermouth (which may be imaginary)

paring of lemon peel or an olive

Take a paring of lemon rind, snap it (yes, if your lemon is fresh, it should snap) so that it almost breaks in half to release the oils in the skin (you could wipe this round the edge of the glass, too), drop into the drink, et voilà. Some prefer to leave out the lemon and add an olive instead.

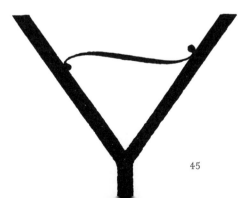

My martini

My perfect martini is Plymouth gin, stirred with ice, Noilly Prat smeared round the rim but none in the drink, and a twist of lemon. I also like a vodkatini made with 6 parts of Belvedere vodka, an almost perfectly soft spirit — its texture is quite incredible, like goose down — to 1 part of vermouth, with an olive and a dash of olive brine, all shaken.

Smoky martini

This takes all the polished power and *3 parts vodka or gin*
dazzle of a martini, and imbues it *¼ part vermouth*
with some of the wilderness of a small *½ part Islay whisky*
Hebridean island. A dash of Islay
whisky is the ingredient that introduces a chorus of wood smoke, peat, iodine, bladderwrack and sea spray to this otherwise collected drink. One for the fireside, when the wind is howling outside. Needless to say, the gin or vodka should come straight from the freezer.

Put all the ingredients in a cocktail shaker with a lot of ice. Shake hard, then double-strain into a martini glass.

Classic champagne cocktail

1 brown sugar cube
7–8 drops Angostura
  bitters
Cognac
champagne
1 strip orange zest

If you are going to mix champagne with anything, there ought to be a rule: the finished drink must be better than the unadulterated champagne. This might seem obvious, but you only need to think of a Buck's Fizz — insipid, apologetic, limp — to realize the rule is seldom followed and actually, unless you have such a bad champagne that disguising the taste entirely is the only way to get it down, almost nothing will improve it.

The champagne cocktail is a glorious exception. The patrician scent of the Cognac conspires with the luxury of the champagne and the tang of the orange peel to make a drink that is heady, celebratory, delicious, and totally and utterly lethal. Even so, I wouldn't waste anything special on this — certainly not vintage, and not even a special non-vintage. A decent supermarket-label fizz is about the right level.

They're easy enough to make. Soak the sugar cube with the Angostura bitters and place in the bottom of a champagne flute. Pour just enough Cognac into the glass to cover the sugar, then top with champagne (be careful; the champagne will froth like fury the moment it hits the sugar) and add the orange zest. Drink at once.

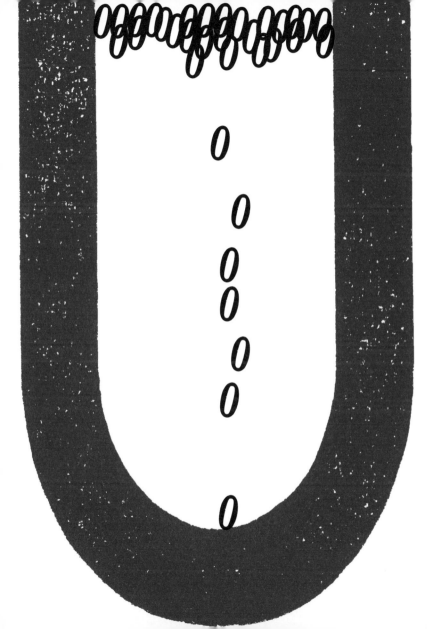

Pousse rapière

1 part Armagnac
1 part Grand Marnier
6 parts champagne
paring of orange
  zest (optional)

Where Cognac is refined and urbane, and smells almost softly soapy, like spicy aftershave, Armagnac has throat and rustic fire. Mixed with fizz, it makes a more feral, jagged version of a classic champagne cocktail. This drink is a take on one they make in Gascony using Pousse Rapière (literally, 'rapier thrust'), a liqueur made from Armagnac macerated with oranges, and sparkling wine. You could use a cheaper sparkling wine instead of champagne.

Pour the first two ingredients into a champagne flute, top with champagne and garnish with the orange zest.

LARGER PARTIES

For larger parties you need drinks that can be turned out very quickly, even if you are distracted by an oven full of devils on horseback that must not be burnt, the doorbell clanging to announce the arrival of a bunch of carol singers and the wrapping of a last-minute Christmas present for someone you forgot. Any finicky preparation is done up front for these drinks. For those who don't know them, devils on horseback are made by wrapping rashers of bacon around prunes and cooking in a hot oven until the bacon is crispy. They are simply delicious, and there's no need to worry about what drink they go with as they won't hang around for long. Of course, you may simply be serving straight fizz, in which case consider making the smoked chicken and caper toasts described on p. 81, and do check my champagne guide on p. 76–9.

Vodka with pomegranate seeds

Jewel-bright, translucent pomegranate seeds look stunning mixed in with ice cubes in a tumbler and then topped with icy vodka. I use a couple of teaspoons of seeds per person, and supply cocktail sticks so you can pick at them when the vodka has gone. Beware, though. Pomegranates are very messy. The first time I tried this, digging into the halved pomegranate to excavate the seeds, I spattered indelible crimson juice in a 360° sweep round my friend's immaculate kitchen. She emailed the next day to say the pristine spines of her cookery books had been 'improved by the Pollocking', but I am not sure she meant it. To avoid such a catastrophe, fill the sink with water, cut the pomegranates in half, submerge and pull apart, scraping the seeds out with your fingers. The debris will separate out and you can harvest the seeds mess-free.

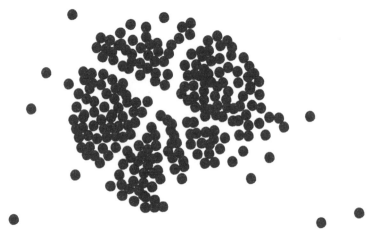

Cheesy biscuits

Everyone has their own variation on the classic cheese-straws recipe. This is mine, adapted from Nigella Lawson's recipe for cheese stars, which uses Red Leicester in place of the Gruyère or Cheddar. I have also added chilli flakes, because I like the sudden burst of heat when you strike one, and thyme. It goes so heavy on the cheese it almost feels as if the flour is there just for propriety's sake, but you get away with it by using self-raising, which helps to puff the biscuits out. How many it makes obviously depends on the size of cutter you use, but it's about right for four to six people. If you like, you can make the dough the day before and leave it, tightly wrapped, in the fridge overnight.

25 g unsalted butter, cold from the fridge

50 g self-raising flour

75 g Gruyère or Cheddar, grated

50 g fresh Parmesan, grated

½ tsp dried chilli flakes

2 tsp fresh thyme leaves, removed from the stalks

1–2 tsp cold water, if you need it

Preheat the oven to 200°C/gas mark 6. Cut the butter into cubes with a knife and rub into the flour and grated cheese with your fingers, as you would to make pastry, until the mixture resembles fine breadcrumbs. Sprinkle the chilli flakes and thyme over the mixture and stir. Once they are thoroughly distributed, use your hands to squeeze and then knead the ingredients into a dough. If necessary, you can add a tiny amount of water, but you shouldn't need it. When you've got it pressed into a ball, wrap the dough tightly in a plastic bag or cling film and leave to rest for 15 minutes in the fridge. Roll the dough out on a floured surface into sheets about 3 mm thick. Use Christmassy cutters — trees, stars, snowmen, reindeer — to cut out the biscuits and spread on to greased baking trays lined with greaseproof paper. Cook for 10 minutes or so, until golden, transfer to cooling racks and serve just as soon as you can touch them — they are delicious hot.

Wintry bellini
The fizz-based cocktail is the perfect drink for large parties, and not just because a full flute with tiny beads of air rushing to the surface always looks and feels the part. These drinks are easy to make, and when you're adding strong flavours, such as Aperol (an Italian bitter similar to Campari) or sloe gin, you can get away with using a much cheaper sparkling wine than you might use if you were serving it neat. The bellini — a Venetian cocktail made from white peach purée and prosecco — is the classic, but that drink belongs in the summer. Here are a few suggestions for more wintry ways with fizz. The Veneziano really does work best with prosecco, but for the rest you can try cava, or other sparkling wines as you please. The one thing you mustn't use is champagne — its yeasty taste gets in the way.

Veneziano

Known in Venice as uno spritz, this can *1 part Aperol*
be made with white wine and sparkling *1 part sparkling water*
water or prosecco (sometimes with, *4 parts prosecco*
sometimes without a little water) and
one of a number of bitters from Campari to Aperol. It's
also catching on as a favourite aperitivo elsewhere in Italy.
I drank it beside the ski slopes of the Alto-Adige where the
preferred combination was Aperol, prosecco and a splash
of soda water, and it was known in every après-ski bar as
the Veneziano. There, it was drunk in a much more diluted

form than the spritz you find in Venice, and it's that version I reproduce here, as it's more appropriate to parties. You can find Aperol in specialist shops, or bring it back from Italy. It has an abv of just 11%, which makes this a very light cocktail. Mix all the ingredients in a glass or a jug.

Cava-Calva

1 part Calvados
1 part fresh apple juice
8 parts sparkling white wine

Here the heady taste of apple brandy is fleshed out with a bit of fresh, sweet apple juice. Robust cava works well here, but you could use any sparkling wine.

Mix the Calvados and apple juice in a glass or jug. Add the sparkling wine and you're ready to go.

Sloe gin fizz

1 part sloe gin
3 parts sparkling white wine

An easy way to enjoy two good things: fizz and English sloe gin. Mix together in a flute or jug and serve. See p. 33–4 for more on sloe gin.

Victoria plum

A purée made from cinnamon-stewed plums tastes as opulent as it looks, staining the sparkling wine a regal purple. Even the hardest of plums can be recruited for this; you just might need to boil them a little longer. I make a job lot of purée and eat the remainder for breakfast with yoghurt. You get about 350–400 ml out of this. I'm afraid the name isn't a reference to the kind of plum you should use; I've named it after myself.

For the purée:
400 g plums
3 rounded tbsp sugar
½ cinnamon stick
100 ml water
1 allspice berry,
   lightly crushed

For the drink:
1 part plum purée
3½ parts sparkling
   wine

To make the purée, use a sharp knife to cut through the plums as if you're going to halve them. If they're soft enough to come apart and you can get the stone out, then do it. Otherwise just score into the fruit as far as the stone, all the way round. Put the plums in a pan with the sugar, cinnamon stick, water and allspice berry. Heat gently, then simmer with a lid slightly displaced to allow some steam to escape, for about 10 minutes or until the plums are soft enough to be squashed. Leave to cool. Sieve the mixture, using the back of a spoon to push the flesh through the mesh.

Mix the plum purée and sparkling wine together — be warned that the wine will fizz furiously when it hits the purée — in a glass or jug and serve.

Campari and clementine

1 part Campari
6 parts freshly
  squeezed clementine
  juice

As every lover of Campari knows, orange is a classic mixer for this Italian bitter. Squeezing fresh clementines does take time, but their juice tastes spicier and more ample and gives a Christmassy tweak to this drink. You can expect to get about 100 ml of juice from 3–4 clementines. I like to make this a long, more refreshing drink, but obviously you could dilute to whatever proportion pleases you the most. Squeeze the clementine juice in advance, and keep it in the fridge until it's needed. If you really want to speed things along you can make up jugfuls of Campari and juice, then simply pour straight over ice.

Pour the Campari into an ice-filled tumbler. Add the clementine juice, stir with a straw to mix and garnish with a thick half-slice of clementine.

Brandy and ginger refresher

1 part Cognac
3 parts ginger ale

There is something very Christmassy about the combined smell of brandy and ginger. The other beauty of this drink is that it's long, so you can take slightly more thirsty sips than you ordinarily might from another brandy cocktail. Mix both ingredients in a jug then pour into ice-filled tumblers to serve.

Mulled wine

1 bottle red wine

1 glass of either
brandy or port

5 cloves

1 orange, sliced

1 cinnamon stick

1 pinch mixed spice

sugar to taste
(optional)

There seems to be a snooty anti-mulled wine movement gathering pace, which is a shame because, along with the ritual mixing of Christmas cake ingredients in a bucket during October half-term, this is a drink that says to me the season has arrived. I never deviate from the recipe my mother has been using for decades. There's no point using anything other than cheap wine, but it should still be something you would be happy to drink cold. Tempranillo from Spain is one good option, and Chilean merlot works well too, because it's sturdy and fruity but not so distinctive that it can't make a good canvas for the spices. Don't just open the wine and pour it directly into the pan. Check that it's not corked first or you will ruin the entire drink. Serves six.

In a saucepan, gently heat the wine and spirit. Stick the cloves into the orange slices. Add the cinnamon, clove-spiked orange slices, mixed spice and sugar. Simmer for 15 minutes, then serve.

Robbie's wassail cup

6 tsp brown sugar

6 eating apples, cored

100 ml water

250 ml, at least, of sherry

2 litres cider

1 orange studded with cloves at approximately 2 cm intervals

2.5 cm piece of cinnamon stick, no more

5 or 6 allspice berries

¼ tsp grated nutmeg, no more

1 or even 2, wine glasses of cooking brandy

I first drank this one grey, rain-soaked evening between Christmas and New Year. Essentially a sort of mulled cider, it's a refreshing and perhaps more sophisticated alternative to mulled wine. The recipe was put together by my friend Robbie by the simple process of looking several up on the Internet, taking all the bits that seemed essential to a wassail cup, leaving out the ones he didn't like the sound of, and adding a few extras that he did.

The word 'wassail' comes from the Old Norse, *ves heill*, to be in good health, according to the *Oxford English Dictionary*, and has a variety of interrelated meanings, all of them full of goodwill. It may be a 'toast or salutation', a 'festivity when much drinking takes place', a drinking song, a drink, or the practice of going from house to house singing carols.

Wassail cup used to be made in celebration of the apple harvest and thus contains cider and baked apples. It smells very good – a noseful of wintry spices that somehow avoids the nasty tendency some of these drinks have to reek of pot-pourri. It tastes great, too – hot and appley, with a pleasing nip in the throat. Fino is the best sort of sherry, but no need for fancy stuff. Again, with the cider, the general rule is that if you'd drink it cold it will be fine hot. As with most recipes of this type, there's no need to be too precious about ingredient quantities — keep tasting and adjust to your own palate. What you must be careful about, though, is the spice element — too much and you will overpower the drink. This makes about twelve glassfuls. You'd need a very large pan to make a bigger batch but you could cook lots of apples ready, and have two pans on the go at once, one being drunk, the other infusing.

Heat the oven to 170°C/gas mark 3. Put a spoonful of sugar in each apple, then place them in a roasting tin with the water and bake for 20–30 minutes until soft but not too fallen or mushy — you don't want them to disintegrate into the wassail. Meanwhile place all the other ingredients except the brandy in a large saucepan. Bring to the boil, then turn down the heat and simmer gently (with just a few bubbles coming to the surface every so often; if it's too hot, the alcohol will boil off) for about 20 minutes. When ready to drink — taste it to check the spices have infused into the cider — add the apples and cook for 5 more minutes. The idea is that the apples should add flavour to the drink, much as a bay leaf does in stock, but not fall into it. Finally, just before serving, add the brandy and continue heating until the mixture is piping hot again. Use a ladle to fill glass beakers or generous wine glasses. This is good with hard cheeses, and the hot apple taste goes well with mince pies too.

Swedish glögg

250 ml vodka
5 cloves
4 cardamom pods
1 stick cinnamon
1 slice fresh root
  ginger
grated rind ½ lemon
50 g raisins
1 bottle red wine
50 g chopped
  almonds, toasted

There are more recipes for glögg – you pronounce it like Yorkshire people say 'Yeurkshire' – than reindeer in Scandinavia. The first signal that you are drinking glögg, though, is the presence of toasted almonds sprinkled on top of the drink. A delicious, and different, mulled wine.

Put the vodka and all the spices and lemon rind into a bowl and leave to soak overnight. Strain to retain the vodka. Add the vodka to the raisins and wine and heat gently until warm. Sprinkle toasted almonds on top and serve.

DRINKS FOR DRIVERS

I have nothing against drinks that have no alcohol in them. Au contraire. I'd even go so far as to say that you can have more fun at a party as a teetotaller because it's easier to stay on top of the conversation and avoid insulting your fellow guests with a few unfiltered pieces of your mind. The most important ingredient in a non-alcoholic drink is actually just the same as it is in one that does contain alcohol: a little care. It's fine to hand someone a glass and shove them in the direction of the cold tap if they've just burst through the door after completing a long-distance run. Otherwise, a little more ceremony goes a long way: a good glass, proper ice, a slice of orange or whatever to finish it off. Also, teetotallers, even temporary ones, often appreciate drinks that encourage you to sip, not swig, so useful qualities in the ingredients are astringency (from cranberries, or the quinine of tonic), acidity (fresh lemon or lime juice) and fiery heat (ginger).

Cranberry cordial

300 g cranberries, either frozen or fresh
200 ml water
100 g sugar

This home-made cranberry purée tastes fresher and sharper than a bought cordial. It also looks festively jewel-bright in the glass. You can add it to tonic, sparkling or simply tap water to make a long refreshing drink.

It's not just useful as a soft drink either; its concentrated fruit and sappy astringency are needed in the cranberry and clementine cocktail on p. 30. Around Christmas you can find punnets of fresh cranberries in supermarkets and greengrocers, but they're usually available from the freezer compartments of supermarkets all year round as well.

Put the ingredients in a saucepan on a medium heat. Bring to a boil, then turn down and simmer for 2 minutes. Turn off the heat, allow the mixture to cool slightly (if you don't let it cool a little, it will spit all over you when you use the blender) and then blitz to a purée using either a hand blender or a food processor. Strain the purée through a fine-mesh sieve into a jug to remove the seeds. It should be quite thick and very smooth. This will keep in the fridge for a couple of weeks. Dilute to taste and serve with ice and thick half-slices of orange.

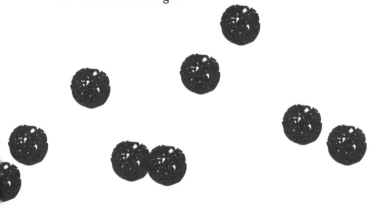

Red grapefruit and elderflower fizz

The gentle smell of white elderflower blossom has become hugely popular in soft drinks. Here it marries so well with the blood grapefruit that you would swear there was a third, hidden, ingredient providing extra complexity.

100 ml elderflower cordial
200 ml red grapefruit juice
800 ml fizzy water

I first drank this at a friend's birthday party at a point in the evening when a long, non-alcoholic drink seemed a sensible idea and it tasted so good that before long half the other guests had abandoned their martinis to move on to this too.

Pour the elderflower cordial into a jug. Add the grapefruit juice, then the fizzy water, stir and then pour into ice-filled glasses.

Pavlovian G&T

You still get the satisfying clatter of ice in a sturdy tumbler, the pfft of the tonic can as it's opened and the gentle crackling fizz as it is poured over the ice.

4 or 5 ice cubes
1 small can of tonic
½ thick slice lemon

All we need is for someone to make a juniper infusion and we'd hardly notice the absence of gin at all. Well, perhaps a bit. Anyway, I find that T without the G is a very good way to make non-drinkers fit in, rather than having them stand clutching a Belisha beacon of orange juice so that everyone else naggily asks why they don't have a proper drink.

Put the ice in a chunky tumbler. Add the tonic, squeeze

the lemon slightly over the drink to release a few drops of juice, drop it into the tonic and you're done.

Fresh, vodka-less Bloody Mary

4 medium tomatoes
5 drops of Tabasco
pinch of salt
1 very small dash of Lea & Perrins
1 squeeze (about 1 tsp) of fresh lemon juice

The flavours in a Bloody Mary are similar to those in steak tartare, only here you put the tomatoes, Tabasco and Lea & Perrins in a glass and serve the meat on the plate. Using fresh tomato juice gives it more delicacy, so go easy on the seasoning. You need the best tomatoes you can find, as the drink depends on them tasting of something.

Blanch the tomatoes for 30 seconds in a bowl or pan of boiling water, then use a sharp knife to score a cross in the skin at the base of each and slip the skin off. On a plate (rather than a board, because you are going to need to recycle the juice that runs off) halve the tomatoes, cut out the stem and discard. Deseed, roughly chop the flesh and put it in a jug. Now hold a strainer over the jug and tip the gubbins from the plate into it so that the runny juice goes in the jug and you hold out the seeds. Blitz the tomatoes with a hand blender until smooth. Now season with the remaining ingredients, tasting as you go. Stir and serve.

Long lemon, lime and ginger

There are so many different ways of using ginger and citrus fruit to flavour a drink. In this one, you make a syrup from the peel and root, then add the lemon juice and the mint only once it is cooled to maximize the freshness. It's an intriguing interplay of ingredients, the ginger contributing a fair bit of fire while the mint cools and the citrus brings brightness.

1 lemon
1 lime
1 chunk ginger root,
*   about 3 cm*
50 g sugar
750 ml boiling water
2 sprigs mint

Pare the zest of the lemon and the lime, being careful not to catch any bitter white pith, and put in a heatproof jug. Peel the ginger root and either chop very finely or grate until you have one rounded dessertspoon of little bits of ginger root. Add this to the jug with the lemon and lime peelings. Add the sugar. Pour in the boiling water, stir and leave to steep until the mixture is cold. Now sieve the whole lot and discard the peel and ginger. Squeeze half the lemon and add the juice to the mixture along with a couple of sprigs of mint. Pour into ice-filled tumblers as and when required.

Spicy apple juice

1 litre apple juice
150 ml water
5 cloves
2 allspice berries
a few gratings of
 nutmeg
½ cinnamon stick

This drink is also good for children, who love the sweetness of apple juice. If you're making mulled cider (Robbie's wassail cup; see p. 60) for the grown-ups you can have this in a pan alongside, which will make them feel involved. For children who don't like spices, serve warm apple juice spiked with blackcurrant cordial instead.

Put all the ingredients into a pan and heat gently. Ladle into glasses as required.

RETRO KITSCH

As Christmas is a time for pulling crackers and wearing silly hats and reindeer jumpers, this might also be the moment to put some slightly more schmaltzy drinks on centre stage.

Snowball

How we all laugh at the very idea of advocaat, the egg and brandy drink that is such a startling, custardy shade of yellow. But guess what. It tastes surprisingly good. You can use it to make a snowball or drink it neat, on the rocks (it's only 17% abv so not too intense). Try it; you may astonish yourself. But please note this should be drunk in the same spirit as one watches a Bond movie re-run.

⅓ part fresh lime juice
1 part advocaat
2 parts lemonade

Pour the lime juice, then the advocaat, then the lemonade into an ice-filled tumbler and stir to mix.

Blood and sand

Perhaps because Mum always used to be given cherry liqueur chocolates for Christmas, the taste of kirsch routes me straight back to Christmas Day, when there were always a box of Black Magic and bar of cherry chocolate on the sideboard. I hunted for ages for a good

1 part Scotch
1 part red vermouth
1 part cherry liqueur
1 part freshly squeezed orange juice

cocktail made using cherry liqueur and eventually found this. Apparently it was created in 1922 for the premiere of the film *Blood and Sand* starring Rudolph Valentino, hence the unseasonal name. I make it using Cherry Heering.

Shake all the ingredients with ice, then strain into a martini glass.

Dark and stormy

1 part rum
2½ parts ginger beer
1 lime wedge

I can only humbly apologize to my friends Robbie and David, who introduced me to this, for my stupidity in leaving this fine drink out of the original *How to Drink*. It's a piratical drink that combines the caramel and vanilla of rum with fiery ginger beer. Do not be tempted to go chi-chi with the ingredients. An extensive tasting session confirmed that Lamb's Navy Rum and Old Jamaica Ginger Beer are as good as things get, unless you fancy a more intense cocktail and go with Gosling's Black Seal.

Pour the rum into an ice-filled tumbler. Top with ginger beer, then squeeze the lime wedge over before dropping it into the drink.

CHRISTMAS DAY

Christmas morning begins with a slow pad round the house in dressing gown and thick socks. If you are the cook, you might go for an early forage through the kitchen and rootle around in the fridge to check on the bread sauce and turkey. If you have children perhaps a less soothing, pre-dawn start as they rampage downstairs to see if Santa has been. Some start drinking perilously early on Christmas Day. This is such a gluttonous period, I prefer to wait until it's almost time to eat, though I have been known to be tempted by a relatively light glass of riesling during morning present-unwrapping. Wine and champagne are the stars of the day, but I have included a cocktail aperitif here in case you do want to open with something a little stronger. Of course, you could make a classic champagne cocktail (see p. 48) or indeed any of the other drinks from 'Glamorous Aperitifs for Small Numbers' (see p. 29–50) instead.

CHRISTMAS DAY APERITIF

For many years, this was the drink my dad made each Christmas using a bottle of Pineau des Charentes – a luscious mixture of unfermented grape juice *1 part Pineau des Charentes* *4 parts champagne* and Cognac – brought back from the previous summer's holiday close to La Rochelle on the western coast of France. He used to joke that, because it was sweet, his mother would gulp it down all the more quickly and become sufficiently pacified to agree that noon was not an appropriate time to eat the heaviest meal of the year. It's not easy to find Pineau des Charentes in this country. Try Nicolas, or Yapp Brothers (yapp.co.uk), though theirs tends to be too good to adulterate. You can get away with a pretty ordinary champagne.

Pour the Pineau des Charentes into a flute and top with champagne.

HOW TO CHOOSE CHAMPAGNE YOU WILL LIKE

There they are, clamouring for attention, every Christmas: the bottles of bubbles, from insanely discounted supermarket own-label to the smart names we all recognize. The range is vast and yet, partly because few of us drink champagne very often and partly because we're bewildered and beguiled by promotions, not to mention preconceptions, stopping to think about how the wine in the bottle tastes, and what we like, can be the last thing we do. Here's a short guide to help steer you through the champagne mists.

The **three champagne grapes** are chardonnay, pinot noir and pinot meunier. Chardonnay (the only white one) brings breadth, creaminess and femininity. It also has very immediate impact, surging up straight away to say hello. Pinot noir (black) is tighter and sappier and has more thrust. You smell it as woodland fruit, and it begins gently, then builds strongly to a crescendo in the mouth. Pinot meunier (also black) is the myrrh and frankincense of a bottle of champagne. It delivers spice and a fragrant, incense-like quality. A champagne might be made from one, two or all of these grapes, in varying proportions, depending on what style the winemaker is after. **A black label** is often (but not always) a clue that there might not be any chardonnay in the wine. Look for the words 'Blanc de Noirs' ('white of blacks'), which mean it's been made from black grapes. A 'Blanc de Blancs' is made from chardonnay only.

Geek information: it's rare to find champagne that is 100 per cent pinot meunier, though cult producer Egly-Ouriet makes one called Les Vignes de Vrigny. It's also unusual to find chardonnay and pinot meunier without pinot noir, and in my view this combination doesn't work: you get a big, puffed-up wine that sits there like a pudding.

Want to test your own taste? Bollinger NV is usually made from about two-thirds pinot noir and has a faint smell of sour cherries as well as a powerful drive. Charles Heidsieck Brut Réserve NV and Pol Roger NV White Label tend to be evenly balanced between the three grapes.

The bubbles come from the carbon dioxide that's released as a by-product of the secondary fermentation the wine undergoes while it's in the bottle. **That yeasty taste**, sometimes described as brioche or sourdough, develops as the wine is left on its lees (dead yeast cells). It's one of the qualities that distinguish champagne from sparkling wines made by other methods. Before you drink it, those dead cells need to come out, so the bottle is gradually turned and inverted, a process called remuage, or riddling, so the debris collects in its neck. This can then be removed (a process called disgorgement), usually by freezing the wine in the neck of the bottle, then releasing the seal so the pellet of wine and sediment flies out under the pressure of the gas in the wine. Most 'brut' champagne isn't **perfectly dry**. After the wine's been disgorged, the bottle needs to be topped up. This is done with a mixture of wine and sugar syrup that determines how sweet the finished wine will be. A bottle of brut can have residual sugar of up to 12 g per litre.

There's a bit of a fashion at the moment for **zero-dosage** (so-called because no dose of sugar is added) champagnes. Champagne is a high-acid wine, and without softening sweetness it can taste very austere. If you're a champagne aficionado you might enjoy its thrillingly clean lines. Advocates of the style often point out that adding the maximum amount of sugar is a way of airbrushing the wrinkles out of bad wine. It's certainly true that a drier style is more revealing, and that those cut-price cheapies you spot in the supermarket will almost certainly be dosed with as much sugar as is legally possible to make them taste crowd-pleasing and plump. Zero-dosage champagne also develops differently in the bottle, but this is not an issue unless you're buying for the cellar. Have a look at Ayala Brut Nature NV or Larmandier-Bernier Terre de Vertus NV if you want to taste a good example of one of these ultra-dry styles.

A handful of favourite brands for a good bottle of NV: Pol Roger, Taittinger, Le Mesnil, Louis Roederer, Charles Heidsieck, Jacquesson, Bollinger, Pierre Gimonnet, Ayala, Chartogne-Taillet, Fleury, Philipponnat.

Geek information: the letters RM on a label, usually in tiny font, stand for récoltant-manipulant – a 'grower champagne', as opposed to one made by a big house using bought-in grapes.

CHRISTMAS FOOD WITH DRINK

To my mind, the best Christmas trees are those decorated in clashingly bad taste. I don't like to see thick swags of colour-coordinated tinsel and identical baubles. I want the battered old cardboard box to come down from the attic and for the tree to be dressed in the foil and egg-carton bells Mum made to save money when she and Dad first married; white lights that break every year before miraculously re-illuminating; hand-painted balls picked up on distant travels; chocolate Babushkas; wooden reindeer; garish baubles . . . What we eat and drink on Christmas Day feels as if it shares the same eclectic, all-embracing spirit. Christmas food and drink is a greedy and unruly collection of family memories and favourites, new and old, all jammed together so that no one and nothing is left out. That said, the classic combinations aren't always, in my view, the best. Turkey with trimmings isn't particularly good with the claret so many people serve, and though it might be the most generous and a great mood-setter, champagne isn't necessarily the perfect thing to drink with smoked salmon. That said, I'm a great believer in doing exactly what you want, and Christmas Day ritual is so much more important than taste that the following might seem almost redundant unless, perhaps, one of them turns out to be the new thing you try this year and ends up being loved so much it is incorporated into the feasting for the next decade or more. Here's hoping . . .

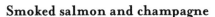

Smoked salmon and champagne

The instant a plate piled up with brown bread and pink smoked salmon is in view I long for someone to put a gently fizzing flute of champagne into my hand. This is mostly because I like champagne, and like smoked salmon, and you would have quite a job wrestling either from my clammy grasp. It isn't the most natural combination though. Champagne is actually more delicious with chicken. It might not be the best idea if you're having turkey for dinner, but for parties at other times, or if the main event is beef, say, you could give it a try. To make a pass-round plate of food, top small pieces of sourdough toast with a mixture of chopped-up smoked chicken breast, capers, torn basil leaves and half low-fat yoghurt, half full-fat mayonnaise. Alternatively, try your smoked salmon with high-quality sauvignon blanc, with which it goes particularly well: think European-style, with a sharp blade of acidity to cut through the oily texture of the fish, no boisterous or fat fruit but instead keen, lean, crisp citrus and grass licking through as cleanly as a squeeze of lemon. Smoked salmon is also good with the lime-leaf-edged curl of Alsatian riesling. As for hot smoked salmon, eaten on white toast smeared with creamed horseradish (which is what we always have on Christmas Day), an aged Australian semillon is a revelation. Semillon is a white grape that can smell of toast and the inside of a new leather handbag even when it hasn't been near a barrel, and there's a smokiness to one with a few years' bottle-age that sits extraordinarily well with the hot horseradish and soft, smoky flakes of fish.

Turkey and pinot gris. Or gamay. Or even pinot noir
Cranberry sauce. Devils on horseback. Chipolata sausages. Maple syrup parsnips. Bread sauce. Apricot and almond stuffing. Carrots. Roast potatoes. Gravy. Turkey. Parmesan cream sprouts. Chestnuts. And you think there might be a wine that can flatter all that at once? Well, there are a couple of grapes that have a jolly good go. Neither of them is found in claret, which I've often been poured with Christmas dinner, but if claret works for you in that 'it's what I want to drink more than anything else' kind of way, then don't let me stop you. If you would like to try a white that will take some of the dryness off the turkey, and act as a gently fruity and aromatic canvas that the cacophony of other dishes can play off, then try a just-off-dry-pinot gris. A medium-to-light-bodied red, such as a bright, refreshing Beaujolais cru (made from gamay), also works well because it isn't thrown off its stride by all the fruit. Pinot noir, from either a more lush Burgundy vintage or the New World, also goes down well. We always eat turkey, not so much because everyone loves it as because it's the only time of year that you do, and we all adore the bits and pieces that go with it, so I've had years of dinners to test these theories out.

Goose and claret

An impeccably turned out young red Bordeaux, its patrician tannic structure as precisely cut as good tailoring, is very good with goose. This is a fatty meat and clean tannic lines, with decent acidity, slice nicely across that. It doesn't have to be claret; you could go Bergerac (for a more rustic, brown brogues feel), or for a white, look for an aged European riesling with lots of texture and emerging kerosene.

Christmas pudding and Moscato d'Asti

Anyone who reaches the pudding stage of Christmas dinner without losing momentum is doing quite well. Anyone who does so and opens a heavy, sticky wine to drink with it deserves a bad attack of gout. Moscato d'Asti might be (unfairly) unfashionable, but this light, faintly effervescent, fresh-grapes-and-blossom sweet white from northern Italy is the perfect antidote to a high-density pudding packed with fruit and nuts. It works because it offers relief, refreshing the mouth and leavening the journey to an overstuffed stomach.

Blue Stilton and port (or have you thought of Madeira?)
Vintage or LBV port is the traditional match for Blue Stilton, but there is a clash between the tannin in the sweet wine and the blue vein in the cheese. It's quite a pleasing clash, and both are high-volume flavours so neither drowns the other out. The wine that counterpoints Blue Stilton really well, though, is an aged Madeira — ideally one made from either bual or malvasia grapes, which will be at the sweeter, heavier, nuttier, dried fig and prunes end of the Madeira scale and sits more smoothly with the cheese. As for port, it is ultra-delicious with chocolate — think chocolate torte, chocolate mousse cake, chocolate truffles, a rich plain chocolate mousse. . .

Mince pies and a glass of — what?
The raisin and citrus peel filling of a mince pie (or a strudel) is very rich, particularly when encased in all that pastry. It demands to be met with a wine that is equally sweet and viscous. An extremely sweet riesling — a beerenauslese or ice wine — of which each drop contains an explosive intensity of honeyed lime peel and cooked apple goes very well. And, though it's a bit more recherché, so does Moscato di Pantelleria, a sweet wine from the volcanic island of Pantelleria, with its black lava rocks, that sits just off the coast of Sicily.

1 packet trifle sponges
  (avoid Tesco's own
  brand, which don't
  taste good)
6–7 fl oz pale
  cream sherry
1 tbsp good red jam —
  raspberry is best
1 pint pink blanc-
  mange, made up
  from a packet mix
1 pint Bird's custard
½ pint double cream

Grandma Moore's sherry trifle

Christmas isn't Christmas without a large helping, or six, of my late Grandma Moore's fabulous old-fashioned sherry trifle, with its luminous layers of pink blancmange, Bird's custard, and hundreds and thousands leaking their colour into the double cream on top. Sounds a trifle odd? The recipe comes from the era of corned beef and tongue sandwiches, but I promise it's gorgeous, especially after a turkey sandwich supper. It makes enough for a hungry family of four to eat twice.

Break the sponge fingers into the bottom of a large glass bowl. Add the sherry bit by bit, sprinkling it across all the sponges — they should be sodden but not afloat. Add the jam, stir gently until it resembles, as my mother puts it, 'a soggy mess', and spread it in a layer across the bottom of the bowl. Make up the blancmange, cool slightly, then pour over the sponge mixture to form a second layer. Leave to cool and set. Now make a pint of custard following the instructions on the tin, but adding a fraction more powder, so it is slightly stiffer than usual. Allow the custard to cool as much as you dare before it sets, then pour it over the blancmange. Refrigerate, and when ready to serve whip the cream and spread over the custard to form the final layer of the trifle. These days we no longer sprinkle with hundreds and thousands, but if you do use them, only add them at the last minute as the colour will bleed into the cream

CREAM
CUSTARD
BLANCMANGE
JAMJAMJAMJAM
SHERRY
SPONGE

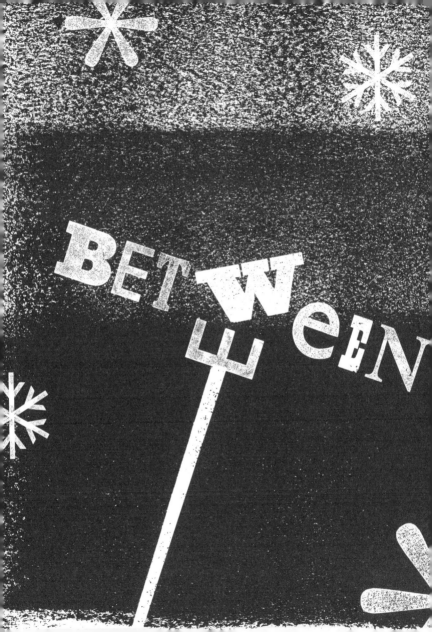

BETWEEN

FEAStS

The lull between Christmas and New Year can come to feel like a week of wintry Sundays, filled with morning forays out into the cold to make the most of the daylight, muffled up in scarves, hat and gloves, followed by cosy afternoons in. There may be a temptation for something creamy and warm to replace energy lost on a long expedition outdoors, or for something medicinal round about afternoon tea time (try a whisky mac). Or there may be the need for soothing lemon and honey to banish the symptoms of a cold, or a tot of spirit to finish off a late evening of armchair discussions.

IN FROM THE COLD: WARMING UP AFTER WALKS ACROSS FROZEN FIELDS

Ginger wine

Ginger wine is made by fermenting currants or raisins, then adding various spices such as cloves and saffron and, of course, the eponymous ginger. People often talk about 'green ginger wine', which has nothing to do with its colour (though it is usually sold in racing-green bottles) and everything to do with the old culinary habit of referring to fresh ginger as green ginger. The name has stuck, even though ground ginger is often used to make it today. The two biggest and best-known brands are Crabbie's, which has some of the sharpness of biting into crystallized stem ginger, and Stone's (who use ground ginger), which by comparison tastes more like baked gingerbread.

This traditional British drink is lovely neat but it is also famously used in a whisky mac.

Whisky mac

This is one of those cocktails that, *2 parts blended* by virtue of a cosy name and warm *whisky* demeanour, somehow have honorary *1 part ginger wine* cup-of-tea status and are considered harmless enough to drink before the sun is quite over the yardarm. Just mix the whisky and ginger wine and pour over ice into a small tumbler.

Applebuie

100 ml cloudy apple juice
100 ml hot water
30 ml Drambuie
1 cinnamon stick

Drambuie is a whisky-based liqueur that here adds fire and spice to hot apple juice and water: a drink that feels almost as thirst-quenching as it is comforting and which takes no more than 2 minutes to prepare. Heat the apple juice in a pan or microwave. Combine it with the hot water and Drambuie in a large glass tumbler or mug and stir with a cinnamon stick until it's as spicy as you'd like it to taste. If making this for several people stick to one cinnamon stick put in the apple juice as it heats.

Spice and coffee milk

Makes two:
400 ml milk
1 clove
2 allspice berries, lightly crushed
2.5 cm cinnamon stick
few gratings of nutmeg
1 cardamom pod, lightly crushed
30 ml strong espresso coffee

The idea here is not to make a spiced coffee, but spiced milk in which coffee acts not as the main flavouring but one of a chorus of spices. I use strong leftover coffee that's been hanging around in my stovetop Moka.

Put the milk and all the spices except the cardamom pod into a small saucepan. Heat gently, without boiling. When the milk is just below simmering point switch off the heat and leave for 10 minutes to steep. Now add the crushed cardamom pod (this goes in last because otherwise the cardamom element will be too strong), leave for another minute or two, reheat the milk until just below simmering point, strain into cups, stir in the coffee and serve.

Milk and plain hot chocolate

200 ml milk
15 g milk chocolate
15 g plain chocolate

Hot chocolate is the perfect antidote to grisly, creepingly damp weather or bone-freezing cold. A bowl of the rich creamy drink can lighten the black hole of one of those mornings that feel as if they will never see the dawn, and it makes a comforting bedtime drink. After years of veering between using milk or plain chocolate I have retreated to the fence and now use both. The plain contributes depth and intensity, the milk easeful luxury.

Heat the milk in a saucepan on the hob, or in a glass jug in a microwave, but don't let it come to the boil. Break the chocolate into pieces and add it to the hot milk, stirring with a wooden spoon until it melts. Pour into a mug and drink.

Some hot chocolate variations

Brandy hot chocolate

There are not many occasions when it feels appropriate to hit the alcohol and hot chocolate at once. After skiing is one of them. If you have been out all afternoon shifting a heavy snowfall from the drive with a shovel, or chopping logs, you may feel you have earned this treat too. Simply add a slug of Cognac or Armagnac or a Spanish brandy to the hot chocolate once it's in the mug, stir to mix and off you go.

Chilli hot chocolate

The Mayans added chilli to drinking chocolate, and the combination of heat with sweetness works extremely well. This tastes best if you make the drink with plain chocolate only. Simply cut a red chilli (its fruity warmth works better than the grassy, less ripe flavour of a green one) in half and discard the seeds. Add the half-chilli to the milk pan as you heat the milk and allow to steep for a few minutes. Remove, add the plain chocolate and continue as normal.

With a blanket of double cream

This is fabulously rich and indulgent. You really need to be making hot chocolate for two to make the beating of the double cream worthwhile. Using about 100 ml double cream for two people, pour the cream into a small bowl and whisk with a balloon whisk until it's stiff. Make the hot chocolate in the usual way, and then once it's in the mug or bowl float spoonfuls of the whipped cream on top. I sometimes stir a teaspoon or two of maple syrup into the cream as an added variation. It sounds horribly sickly, but if you're hungry it's surprising how good it tastes.

Drinks to chase away a cold

Sniffles and sore throats are rife at this time of year, yet look at the small print on the bottles of cough syrup on the chemist's shelf and you'll find many contain little more than glucose, sucrose, honey and alcohol. Better to take the fresh ingredients and make a cheaper, more delicious, longer drink at home.

Lemon, honey and hot water

Just mix the freshly squeezed lemon *juice of ½–1 lemon*
juice and honey in a glass or mug, then *1 tsp honey*
top with water that's recently boiled but
just cooled a little. My taste is generally quite sour, so you may need to double or even treble the quantity of honey. The result feels throat-repairing (even if only temporarily) and easily does instead of tea at breakfast time.

Hot toddy

Of course, lemon, honey and hot water is even more 'medicinal' if finished off with a tot of whisky. The vitamin C for health, the honey to soothe, the alcohol to numb . . .

Hot buttered rum

1 thin slice of butter
1 tsp brown sugar
1 generous tot of dark rum
1 cinnamon stick
nutmeg (optional)

This has a real security-blanket feel to it. Mix the butter in a glass with the brown sugar and add the rum, then top with hot water and drop in the cinnamon. Add a tiny grating of nutmeg if you like to finish.

Eggnog

It was snuffling round the leftovers on Boxing Day that got me into this. I'd eaten a few cold sausages and a couple of potato croquettes, but what I really had my eye on was the brandy sauce left over from the pudding. Would it be acceptable to drink it straight from the jug? Well, no one was looking . . . That's when it crossed my mind that eggnog — at its simplest a combination of raw eggs, brandy, milk and perhaps some cream — is nothing more than raw custard spiked with alcohol. Why had I always been so put off by the idea? It is particularly suited to cosseting you through the sort of dark weekend afternoons when you're in a dressing gown pretending to be far more under the weather than you actually feel, not eating very much and not intending to leave the house again until Monday. It is also good when there is present wrapping to be done.

Americans are big on eggnog and have dozens of variations on the theme. I like mine with brandy best, and prefer to beat the yolk and white separately, as it gives a better texture. Eggnogs have a comforting nursery feel, probably because they're reminiscent of the mug of hot milk with sugar and an egg stirred in that parents used to feed children before they went to bed, and, perhaps because they feel nourishing, they are dangerously easy to gulp back.

This recipe makes two restrained portions or a single very greedy one, so serve either in a pair of small tumblers or wine glasses, or in a tall Collins glass.

Beat the egg yolk with half the sugar until the colour pales. Whisk the egg white until it stiffens, add the remaining sugar and whisk to glossy soft peaks. Combine the milk, cream, spirit and egg yolk mixture. Fold in the egg white, pour into glasses and top with grated nutmeg or flakes of cinnamon stick if you feel like it (I never do).

1 egg, separated
25 g caster sugar
175 ml milk
50 ml double cream
30 ml brandy or rum
nutmeg or cinnamon
   (optional)

M M M M

Brandy Alexander

1 part brandy
1 part crème de cacao
1 part double cream

Cream cocktails are not everyone's bag but sometimes, after a light supper, say, the sweetness is just what you need. The only bad thing about this classic is that it calls for crème de cacao, cocoa bean liqueur, which all too easily becomes one of those nuisance bottles that fill your cupboard and are taken out only once or twice a year, so ensure you really like it before you make the investment.

Shake all the ingredients with ice and strain into a cocktail glass.

A SIP OF SOMETHING BY THE FIRE

A word on whisky

Whisky is a spirit to which I always come with a sense of reverence. This is not just because of the taste, in which you find hints of the icy sea spume and peat bogs of the wild landscape in which it is made. It's also because, of all drinks, this is the one I associate either with hard drinking and hard men or with serious conversation and contemplation. No doctor I have spoken to has ever been able to confirm the suspicion many of us hold that different drinks affect our brain in different ways, so perhaps the reverse is true: we turn to certain drinks according to our mood. If you were hoping to set the world to rights over a late-night drink, a decent Scotch might well be something you would pour. It certainly feels appropriately intellectual: a drink you can wrestle with, linger over and appreciate with all its nooks and crannies.

Apparently Jeremy Paxman sometimes likes to 'come down' after his *Newsnight* interrogations with a couple of glasses of whisky — always blends, Cutty Sark or Bell's, I was told: 'He can't be doing with single malts. He'd be like a spinning top which always takes ages to settle.' Quite so. It wouldn't feel right to hear he was drinking peach schnapps, or pinot grigio. The reverse is also true: imagine settling down with a tumbler of whisky and turning on *Wheel of Fortune*.

There is a historical association between whisky and

thinkers and writers, many of whom drank to excess. Dylan Thomas's last words are said, apocryphally perhaps, to have been, 'I've just had eighteen straight whiskies, I think that's the record.' Winston Churchill and Graham Greene were also keen whisky drinkers. Greene wasn't always pernickety about flavour, though. In his novel *The Human Factor* he has the double agent Maurice Castle drink J&B whisky, thebetter to be secretive about the level of his alcohol consumption. 'He always bought J&B because of its colour,' writes Greene. 'A large whisky and soda looked no stronger than a weak one of another brand.'

Whisky drinkers are usually more precise in their likes and dislikes. They know exactly what mood will suit a blend (which is composed from both barley and grain whiskies that may come from dozens of different distilleries), are precise about when they will have a vatted malt (made only from malted barley but a blend from several distilleries), or when only a single malt (a whisky made from malted barley in a single distillery) will do.

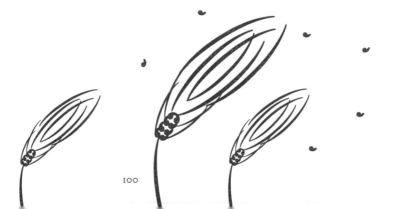

They will also have run their palates across the heather-covered hills, the glens and the craggy coastlines of the Scottish landscape and worked out which area makes malts that please them the most. They will be aware that Islay, the southernmost island of the Inner Hebrides, is famed for the pungent, iodine-like, smoky peat smell of its whiskies; that the Lowlands produce some of the most delicate and floral; that Speyside in the east of the mainland is said to produce some of the most complex. And they will know about the imprint that the oak, whether it is an old sherry cask or a bourbon barrel, will leave on the spirit.

For the whisky drinker, there is very much to consider — it is a subject that requires an entire volume of its own. Suffice here to say that when you are drinking whisky, one of the choices you will have to make is how: straight up, on the rocks or with a little cold water. I usually go with water, which I serve on the side in a small milk jug so that people can pour their own, because woe betide you if you get it wrong in someone else's glass. The reason is that water, not being as cold as ice, allows you to taste the spirit better, and diluting it slightly does seem to make the flavour bloom and express itself more eloquently.

A handful of my favourite whiskies, a list that grows longer every time I taste more, would include the following: Highland Park Twelve Years Old, a heathery, sophisticated, beautifully defined Orkney single malt; Ardbeg Ten Years Old, an Islay with a smoky, marine tingle and satisfying sense of completeness; and the Macallan Sherry Oak 10 Years Old, for the spicy, panforte-like, Christmassy feel the sherry casks bring to the spirit.

Cognac versus Armagnac

Brandy is a spirit distilled from fermented grape juice (though the word is often applied to spirits made from other fruits). It can be made anywhere in the world – I have had some pretty decent stuff from Spain – but the finest comes from France, from two neighbouring regions.

Cognac and Armagnac are like the town mouse and the country mouse of the brandy world. Cognac has the sophistication and finesse of Mr City Souris, as suave as a man in a Savile Row suit, all neatly pressed and ironed into shape. Its smell is smooth and sweetly woody, like continental aftershave, and it seems burnished, like a highly polished antique mirror. Armagnac, the country mouse, is not such an elegant fellow, but he has a lot of character. If he were a piece of furniture, he'd be a solid oak kitchen table, sturdy and beautifully carved, that has been in the family for years, seen a lot of spillages and a lot of raucous dinners, and come out of them intact but not unmarked. Armagnac is not just more rustic, it is throaty. You can feel its guts, the hot fire, almost hear the stories that would be told over a glass of it. You can probably tell that's where my heart is, but the consensus is that Cognac is the finer, leaving Armagnac looking just a little too yokel to compete.

The reasons for the differing taste are several. Cognac is mostly made from the ugni blanc grape, which is known in Italy as trebbiano, and makes quite undistinguished wine (its distillate is clearly a different matter). The Cognac vineyards are in western France, north of Bordeaux, in the Charente and Charente-Maritime, and spill into the Dordogne and Deux-Sèvres. And the spirit is double-distilled, a batch at a time, in a copper-pot still, before being matured in oak, which soaks through the spirit, filling out its flavour.

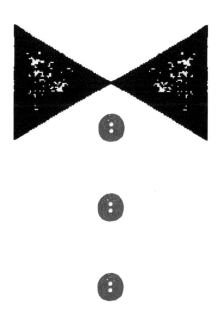

Armagnac is made among the narrow lanes and quiet hills of Gascony, to the south of Bordeaux, very often in tiny quantities by small family producers. It is also made from ugni blanc, but significant amounts of two other grapes, colombard and folle blanche, are also used. It is distilled just once, in a number of different ways, sometimes like Cognac, sometimes in continuous or semi-continuous stills, before it goes into barrels. Armagnac needs years before it gives and softens enough to show its true pedigree, but when you do sip an old one, with its distant flavours of prunes and forests, the extraordinary thing is that it never tastes its age.

As for what to drink it out of, those ostentatious and cumbersome balloon-shaped glasses aren't necessary: brandy likes to be drunk out of a glass that allows some, but not too much, of the drink to evaporate. As ever, you can buy the ideal shape from a specialist, but a good wine glass that curves in at the top will do.

As regards labels, here are a few pointers. Cognac must have been aged in oak for two years before it's released and, in ascending order of quality, it may be marked three star or VS (Very Special, meaning its youngest spirit is at least two years old); VSOP (Very Special Old Pale, meaning the youngest element must be at least four years old); Napoleon, XO or Hors d'Age (youngest element at least six years old). For Armagnac, three star must be more than two years old, VSOP over five and XO over six, but you will frequently come across much older spirits than that.

Blazing brandy with red berries

This opulent combination of juicy *small handful of* red berries with flaming brandy tastes *mixed berries* as good as it looks. I make it with the *50 ml Cognac* 'summer berry' mixtures you find in the freezer compartments of supermarkets. If putting together your own, try to include raspberries, redcurrants and blackberries, perhaps with blueberries and blackcurrants too. This tends to go horribly wrong if you try to make it after a boozy dinner, so be careful.

Put the fruit and brandy in a brandy balloon and leave to steep for a few minutes. If you're using frozen berries, leave a little while longer so the fruit has time to defrost and flavour the spirit. Fill a tumbler with hot water. Balance the brandy glass on top, and turn it slowly so that the glass and the brandy warm up. Keeping the glass tilted so that the brandy almost runs out, and pointing away from you so that you don't set fire to yourself, strike a match and use it to light the surface of the evaporating brandy nearest to the mouth of the glass. Stir until the flame is extinguished and then drink.

There's always a moment when you realize you couldn't so much as look at another turkey sandwich, or even stuff down one more chipolata sausage. Needless to say, this is not the point at which I stop eating and drinking. It is the point at which I go for a change of pace and turn to fresher, sharper, lighter flavours – infusions and tisanes that feel cleansing and hydrating – but also crisp, ice-cold vodka, drunk in bee-sting shots straight from the freezer, infused with cranberries or made into a lychee martini, all of which help to enliven chilly, dark January nights.

PURITANICAL MOMENTS

The following drinks aren't so much for social consumption as for perking you up first thing in the morning, or when you get back from the gym. The watery ones are tastier than you might think.

Rosemary and lemon infusion

Rosemary has such an intense savoury taste that a little bit goes a long way, which is why I make this in a teapot, adding more hot water as I drink my way through it.

1 small sprig rosemary
2 thick slices of lemon, halved
500 ml hot water

Put the rosemary in a teapot. Drop one slice of lemon into the pot; squeeze in the juice of the other and then drop it in too. Add hot water, leave for a few minutes to steep and then pour into small china cups.

Lime zest and ginger infusion

A cleansing alternative to builder's tea or the caffeine-shock of espresso first thing in the morning. The fiery ginger and vibrant lime go well together. Ginger is also thought to help with nausea, particularly morning sickness.

1 large paring lime zest
sliver ginger root
hot water

Put the lime zest and ginger in a mug, pour over water that's just boiled and drink as soon as it's cool enough to sip.

Cucumber and watercress vitamin injection

½ cucumber, roughly chopped
½ small handful watercress, chopped

Most vegetables can't be turned into juice unless you have a juicer. The cucumber is an exception. Adding watercress puts some fire into what would otherwise be an exceptionally gentle drink.

Put the cucumber in a jug and blitz with a hand blender until smooth. Add the watercress and blitz again. Pour into a tumbler with a couple of ice cubes.

Grapefruit and passion fruit

This is an unexpectedly brilliant combination I picked up from a Nigel Slater recipe, though I don't put quite *2 white grapefruits* *1 passion fruit* so much passion fruit in mine as he does. White grapefruit juice has such a bracing, sharp tang that it feels enlivening just to sip it. Adding passion fruit seeds studs it with little bursts of tropicality. A surprisingly delicious combination.

Halve and squeeze the grapefruits and pour the juice into a glass. Halve the passion fruit and use a spoon to scoop the seeds into the glass. Stir to mix.

Pomegranate and orange flower smoothie

This Middle Eastern combination is wonderfully fragrant. Mix all the ingredients together in a large glass, add a cube or two of ice and drink.

100 ml low-fat *yoghurt* *30 ml water* *60 ml pomegranate* *juice* *½ tsp orange* *flower water* *sprinkling of* *pomegranate seeds*

ICE AND SNOW

How rough do you like your vodka?
In November 2006 the BBC's Russian affairs analyst reported that Osman Paragulgov, head of Russia's union of wine and spirit producers, was lobbying for the introduction of something he called 'social vodka': a regulated spirit to feed the appetites of those too poor to buy the real thing.

If this sounds like a dipsomaniac's approach to welfare provision, behind it lay a brutal reality. The previous month a clutch of Siberian towns had announced a state of emergency after nearly 900 people were hospitalized with liver failure after drinking counterfeit vodka. The annual death rate across the country for those poisoned by industrial solvents passed off as vodka was estimated at around 42,000. The question you might ask is why the pungent smell of window-cleaner or anti-rust solution as a glass is raised to the lips does not give the game away. Part of the answer is that often it is not drunk for pleasure but to ease obliteration.

The writer Vitali Vitaliev once spent an evening showing me how to drink vodka 'the Russian way', as he put it, a procedure that involved exhaling, gulping back a shot and downing a mouthful of gherkin or pickled cabbage before inhaling again. This was, he said, the best method of getting the spirit, all too often ferociously harsh, down without tasting it. I couldn't quite decide if he was winding me up when he said that if no pickles were available, it would be acceptable to pick up a scraggy alley cat and bury your nose in its matted fur instead. He also became quite passionate when it was suggested that some of us drink because we actually like the flavour of the stuff we are swallowing. 'Your taste buds have been perverted by the western drinking culture!' he cried.

No doubt Vitaliev would have got on splendidly with Prince Harry, who was once photographed by the tabloids snorting vodka up his nostril, a method of ingestion that ingeniously bypasses the taste buds, thus dispensing with the need for an old moggy. I take the quaint view that if you're going to have a drink, you may as well enjoy it.

Even real vodka can be pretty rough, though. Vodka is a white spirit that is distilled, in some places, from the by-products of oil refining or wood-pulp processing, neither of which sounds delicious. Fortunately EU regulations require it to be made from 'alcohol of agricultural origin'. Complaining that they did not think the drink ought to be an 'alcoholic wastebucket', three countries – Finland, Sweden and Poland – from the so-called 'vodka belt' recently attempted to have this definition restricted to the traditional but not traditionally desperate ingredients of grain and potato. They were unsuccessful: today you can buy vodka made from all sorts of ingredients, from grapes (for example, the French brand, Ciroc, which many argue ought to be a brandy or grappa) to molasses or soya beans.

I think you can sometimes taste what a vodka has been made from: rye, for example, gives a particularly savoury, caraway-like taste, while the molasses used in many cheap supermarket brands give a more throaty spirit with little nuance or precision. But unless the vodka is flavoured, what makes arguably the biggest difference is its purity, achieved by redistilling (and sometimes redistilling again) and filtering.

Up to a point it is a good idea to create vodkas so refined that they don't attack your palate like a pitbull with a man's arm between its teeth, or taste so horrible they are, literally, indistinguishable from industrial solvents. But unless you're going to be drinking the spirit neat, as either a shot or a martini, very pure vodka is not only an expensive way of doing things, it's not even always the best.

In some ways, our modern method of drinking vodka with mixers or as a base for cocktails is not so different to that described by Vitaliev: we merely substitute cranberry juice

for cat fur to mask the taste of the alcohol. But vodka brands have become a fashion statement for which some are willing to pay extortionate prices.

When making cocktails at home, I use brands such as Smirnoff, which might not be exciting neat but are more than good enough for the cocktail job, because they don't have off-flavours that might spoil the balance of the drink, and aren't ludicrously expensive.

If drinking it with tonic (which I rarely do) I go even further and say, almost heretically, the cheaper the better. With tonic water – and I will only accept the best tonic water – I will actually drink the cheapest vodka you can find. Vaguely reminiscent of petroleum? No problem. A slight hint of old potatoes? Perfectly fine. A scraping, fiery texture with a good old burn on the back of the throat? Bring it on. Unless you have something you can taste through the quinine and sweetener in the tonic, what on earth would be the point?

How to taste posh vodka

Tasting vodka is a little like tasting bottled mineral water: it's all about texture and nuance, and it's surprising how much your palate can discern when you are drinking it neat. Some vodkas feel very precise and hard-edged, like a diamond; others feel more splurgy and fluent. Some are silkily soft; others rasp. Some taste like the alcoholic equivalent of tap water that's not obviously chlorinated. That is, you think, 'Yes, it just tastes like vodka, there's no other tasting note.'

I keep two unflavoured vodkas in my freezer for drinking neat or as martinis. One is Russian Standard, which is made from wheat grain and 'pure glacial water from the frozen north' (this guff is unavoidable). It has a smooth texture but a pleasing viscosity – fat and oily, in a good way – and some breadth. It is lovely with raw or smoked fish, and, because of the mouth-feel, works well with fatty fish such as tuna belly. For something lighter, sharper and fresher, I also have Belvedere. This is distilled and bottled in Poland, made from 100 per cent rye grain, which gives it a sharp, caraway breeziness, and it has the softness of finest angora.

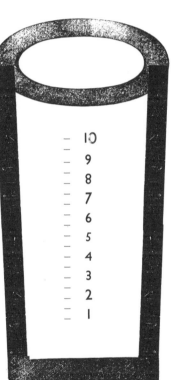

Flavoured vodka

A new era for flavoured vodka was ushered in by the Swedish firm Absolut back in the 1980s, when they launched Absolut Peppar (a spicy flavoured vodka that tastes of chilli, herbs and green tomatoes), which they followed with Absolut Citron, a lemon-flavoured vodka that became instantly fashionable. But flavouring vodka is not new. It will come as no surprise to hear that, to mask the clumsiness of early distilled spirits, the Russians and Poles have been doing it for centuries, using a range of natural ingredients that included acorns, horseradish and watermelon. I sometimes add my own flavourings to vodka (see opposite page if you would like to make cranberry vodka). The one commercial flavoured vodka that stands out from the rest and which I usually have in my freezer is Żubrówka, from Poland. Made from rye, it is infused with bisongrass, otherwise known as sweetgrass, because of its intense perfume, and as Holy Grass by the American Indians. The stuff used to flavour Żubrówka is harvested by hand from the Bialowieza Primeval Forest, a stretch of ancient woodland still relatively undisturbed by humans, and it gives the vodka a sweet meadow scent, as if freshly cut grass and dried grass have been mixed together.

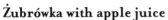

Żubrówka with apple juice

When herbal Żubrówka meets apple juice, an extraordinary fusion happens: it's almost as if you can smell cinnamon, or an apple crumble baking in the oven.

3 parts fresh apple juice

1 part Żubrówka

Pour the apple juice and Żubrówka over plenty of ice. You can also make a longer drink by mixing I part Żubrówka with I½ parts apple juice, then topping with sparkling water. This time, a more herbaceous character comes through — all tarragon and apples — which is lovely with smoked fish if you're looking for a nibble.

Making your own cranberry vodka

Fresh cranberries are always around in the supermarkets just before Christmas and nothing is simpler than making your own cranberry vodka. Just use the butt of a rolling pin lightly to crush a large handful of berries (they should be split but still hold their shape), slip them into a bottle of vodka, leave them to steep for a few days at room temperature, then put the bottle in the freezer. This makes a surprisingly strong-flavoured, pleasingly astringent drink that is delicious drunk icy cold in shot-sized portions.

Scandinavian inspiration: aquavit

Aquavit is hard to find in this country. The Scandinavian spirit is like a herbal vodka: strong, colourless, imbued usually with caraway and sometimes with other herbs such as dill and cumin. With its lethal alcohol and herbaceous bite, it tastes as if it were made for fortifying the soul on serious expeditions, across plains of ice, through landscapes where the only noise is the howling of the wind and the creaking of the snow. If you're bringing a bottle home, look out for Aalborg Akvavit from Denmark in the Duty Free. Keep in the freezer.

Food to eat with neat vodkas and aquavit

With a glass of vodka kept at sub-zero temperatures so that it is not only cold but also viscous, a smorgasbord is delicious. There would have to be blinis – with wild smoked salmon, cod's roe and caviar if you have a wealthy Russian for a friend. There would be herring, crispbread, sliced egg and gherkins and perhaps other kinds of smoked fish and meat. If you are drinking aquavit, the gamey, savoury taste of bresaola that has been cured with dill and juniper goes brilliantly, so I'd be tempted to ditch everything else and simply make a bresaola, lemon and rocket salad as a starter in the ordinary way. If you are going to move on to a main course, then look at recipes that use allspice (a Finnish favourite) – say, meatballs flavoured with allspice and served in a creamy sauce.

Lychee martini

In his *Oxford Companion to Food* Alan Davidson tells us that in China in the first century AD 'a special courier service with swift horses was set up to bring fresh lychees from Canton north to the Imperial Court'. Later, during the Ming dynasty, special lychee clubs met in temples to gorge themselves silly on the fruit so prized that it has moved countless Chinese poets to rhapsodic verse. We don't quite seem to appreciate the lychee in the same way. It is an odd creature: pocked brittle skin that seems to belong to a prehistoric reptile, and slippery, pale flesh that looks a bit like an eyeball torn from its socket. It's the smell that gets you – haunting and fragile, like a nightingale's song. Or at least that's how you start to think after a few lychee martinis. (Strictly speaking it isn't correct to use the term 'martini' for fruit vodka drinks, but it's become common practice to do so, and I've stuck with it because it sounds more appealing.) The concept here is simple: take the fruit, peel, stone, blend, sieve to remove bits of shell and lumps, add about the same amount or slightly more vodka from the freezer, shake with ice and strain into cocktail glasses. You could use tinned lychees, but though they give a more robust drink, there is no refinement. Fresh ones (the ones on the supermarkets shelves in January usually seem to be from Madagascar) have much more fragrance and produce a more ethereal, 'home-made' taste. I like to drink this before eating a bowl of noodles or a fresh stir-fry.

ACKNOWLEDGEMENTS

I am very grateful for the help and wise advice of Joe Wadsack (whose wonderful recipe I pinched), Lizzy Kremer and Sara Holloway.

Very many thanks are also due to the guinea pigs: all those friends who have been dragged into my kitchen, force-fed several different versions of the same drink and managed to remain lucid enough to make helpful observations. I think some of you might have been asked to drink rum daiquiris more than once because the cocktails were so good I kept mislaying the notes telling me what proportions I'd used to make them. Thank you.

cheers

INDEX

advocaat 69

aged rum daiquiri 31

Aperol 20, 54

   Veneziano 55–6

apples and apple juice

   applebuie 92

   Cava-Calva 56

   Robbie's wassail

      cup 60

   spicy apple juice 68

   Żubrówka with apple

      juice 119

aquavit 121

Armagnac 102–104

   pousse rapière 50

beer 19

bellini 54

bitters 20, 54, 55

   Angostura 19, 29, 48

   see also Aperol,

      Campari

blazing brandy with red

   berries 105

blood and sand 69

Bramhope 29

brandy 14, 102–104,

   105

brandy Alexander

   98

brandy and ginger

   refresher 58

eggnog 97

hot chocolate 94

mulled wine 59

Robbie's wassail cup

   60

see also Armagnac,

   Cognac

Buck's Fizz 48

Calvados 56

Campari 20, 54, 55

   and clementine 58

cava 16, 54

   Cava-Calva 56

champagne 17, 18, 51,

   54, 76–9

   choosing 76–9

   Christmas Day

      aperitif 75

   classic champagne

      cocktail 48

   pousse rapière 50

   with food 81

cheesy biscuits 53

cherry liqueur 69–70

   Cherry Heering 70

chicken and caper

   toasts 81

Christmas Day

   aperitif 75

cider 68

   Robbie's wassail

      cup 60

classic champagne

   cocktail 48

clementine juice 29,

   30, 58

coffee 92

Cognac 14, 50, 75,

   102–104

   blazing brandy with

      red berries 105

   brandy and ginger

      refresher 58

   classic champagne

      cocktail 48

   cranberry and

      clementine sour

      30

   H by Hine 14

Cointreau 20

   cranberry and

      clementine sour

      30

   sidecar 44

cordial 19, 65, 68
Bottlegreen Aromatic
Lime 19
Belvoir Elderflower 19
cranberry cordial 63
cranberry 20
and clementine
sour 30
cordial 63
vodka 120
crème de cacao 98
cucumber and watercress
vitamin injection 110
dark and stormy 70
Drambuie 92
eggnog 96–7
fresh, vodka-less Bloody
Mary 66
gin 15, 16, 37, 42–3,
45, 47
and tonic 34–43, 65
Beefeater 42
Berry Bros. & Rudd
16, 43
Gin Mare 43
Gordon's 37
martini 45, 47
Plymouth 47
Sipsmith 42

Tanqueray 15, 37, 42
see also sloe gin
ginger ale 58
ginger beer 70
ginger wine 91
glögg see Swedish glögg
gomme syrup 20, 29,
31, 32
Grand Marnier 50
Grandma Moore's
sherry trifle 86
grapefruit and passion
fruit 111
hot buttered rum 96
hot chocolate 93–5
hot toddy 96
lemons and lemon juice
32, 34–7, 38, 39, 44,
45, 62, 65
hot toddy 96
lemon, honey and
hot water 95
long lemon, lime and
ginger 67
rosemary and lemon
infusion 109
limes and lime juice 29,
31, 34–7, 39, 69, 70
lime zest and ginger

infusion 109
long lemon, lime and
ginger 67
lychee martini 122
Madeira 85
martini 45–7
lychee martini 122
smoky martini 47
milk
hot chocolate 93–5
spice and coffee milk
92
Moscato d'Asti 83
Moscato di Pantelleria
85
Noilly Prat 47
non-alcoholic drinks
63–8, 92–5, 108–11
oranges and orange
juice 20, 42, 48, 59,
60, 64, 69
Pavlovian G&T 65
Pineau des Charentes 75
pomegranate
and orange flower
smoothie 111
vodka with
pomegranate seeds
52

port 59, 85
pousse rapière 50
prosecco 16, 54
  Veneziano 55
red grapefruit and
  elderflower fizz 65
Robbie's wassail cup
  60, 68
rosemary and lemon
  infusion 109
rum 20
  aged rum daiquiri 31
  Bramhope 29
  dark and stormy 70
  eggnog 97
  El Dorado 20, 29, 31
  Gosling's 70
  hot buttered rum 96
  Lamb's 70
Santa Teresa Rhum
  Orange 20
sherry 60
  Grandma Moore's
    sherry trifle 86
sidecar 44
sloe gin 20, 32–4 54
  Gordon's 34
  Hayman's 32, 33
  Plymouth 33

Sipsmith 33
sloe gin fizz 56
sloe gin sour 32
smoked salmon 81
snowball 69
soft drinks see non-
  alcoholic drinks
sparkling wine 50, 57
  Cava-Calva 56
  sloe gin fizz 56
  Victoria plum 57
spice and coffee milk 92
spicy apple juice 68
Swedish glögg 62
tonic water 19, 34,
  37–8, 115
  Fever-Tree 19, 38, 42
  Pavlovian G&T 65
  Schweppes 19, 34,
    37–8
  Waitrose 38
Veneziano 55
vermouth 20
  blood and sand 69
  martini 45, 47
  Noilly Prat 47
Victoria plum 57
vodka 15, 45, 47, 52,
  62, 112–22

Aalborg Akvavit 121
Belvedere 47, 116
Ciroc 113
cranberry and
  clementine sour 30
cranberry vodka 119
flavoured 118
lychee martini 122
Russian Standard 116
Smirnoff 115
Swedish glögg 62
with food 121
with pomegranate
  seeds 52
with tonic 115
Żubrówka 119
vodkatini 45, 47
whisky 15, 47, 96,
  99–102
  Ardbeg 101
  blood and sand 69
  Highland Park 15, 101
  hot toddy 96
  Islay 47, 101
  Macallan 102
  smoky martini 47
  whisky mac 91
wine 16–18
  ginger 91

mulled 59
red 59, 62, 82, 83
sourcing 16–18
Swedish glögg 62
sweet 83, 85
white 81–2
with food 80–5
see also sparkling
      wine, cava,
         champagne,
            prosecco
wintry bellini 54
Żubrówka with apple
   juice 119